There comes a day when the weight of
our experiences, our deeper knowledge
of the world, and the perspective gained
from passing years cause us to stop,
rethink our positions a little, and finally
realize, after all is said and done...

"Dad <u>was</u> right!"

Blue Mountain Arts®

Bestselling Titles

By Susan Polis Schutz:

To My Daughter, with Love, on the Important Things in Life

To My Son with Love

By Douglas Pagels:

42 Gifts I'd Like to Give to You

100 Things to Always Remember... and One Thing to Never Forget

May You Always Have an Angel by Your Side

To the One Person I Consider to Be My Soul Mate

Is It Time to Make a Change?

by Deanna Beisser

To the Love of My Life

by Donna Fargo

Anthologies:

Always Believe in Yourself and Your Dreams

For You, My Daughter

Friends for Life

Hang In There

I Love You, Mom

I'm Glad You Are My Sister

The Joys and Challenges of Motherhood

The Language of Recovery

Marriage Is a Promise of Love

Teaching and Learning Are Lifelong Journeys

There Is Greatness Within You, My Son

Think Positive Thoughts Every Day

Thoughts to Share with a Wonderful Teenager

True Wealth

With God by Your Side ...You Never Have to Be Alone

You're Just like A Sister to Me

Dad Was Right!

Advice from Fathers on Achieving Everything You Want in Life

A Blue Mountain Arts® Collection

Edited by Gary Morris

Blue Mountain Press™

Boulder, Colorado

Copyright © 2005 by Blue Mountain Arts, Inc.

Library of Congress Control Number: 2005921116
ISBN: 0-88396-927-0

ACKNOWLEDGMENTS appear on page 64.

Certain trademarks are used under license.
BLUE MOUNTAIN PRESS is registered in U.S. Patent and Trademark Office.

Printed in the United States of America.
First Printing: 2005

 This book is printed on recycled paper.

This book is printed on fine quality, laid embossed, 80 lb. paper. This paper has been specially produced to be acid free (neutral pH) and contains no groundwood or unbleached pulp. It conforms with all the requirements of the American National Standards Institute, Inc., so as to ensure that this book will last and be enjoyed by future generations.

Blue Mountain Arts, Inc.
P.O. Box 4549, Boulder, Colorado 80306

Contents

Introduction

Mark Twain may have said it best for all of us: "When I was a boy of fourteen, my father was so ignorant I could hardly stand to have the old man around. But when I got to be twenty-one, I was astonished at how much the old man had learned in seven years."

From the beginning of our lives, it seems, we receive an unending supply of information, advice, encouragement, and guidance from our dads and all those other "father figures" we depend on — the uncles, brothers, teachers, and male mentors who are such an integral part of our days. When we're young, we tend to idealize these men and take their words at face value; as we become teenagers and young adults, we end up questioning everything they told us and rejecting much of it in favor of our own ideas and beliefs. Eventually, there comes a day when the weight of our experiences, our deeper knowledge of the world, and the perspective gained from passing years cause us to stop, rethink our positions a little, and finally realize, after all is said and done...

"Dad was right!"

The time comes when we understand that the words he tried to instill in us — "Always go the extra mile," "Money can't buy you happiness," or "Actions speak louder than words" — were not just lessons he had learned through his own experience. More importantly, they represent guideposts on a pretty decent roadmap that can guide us to getting more out of our lives. A lot of those time-tested ideas really do turn out to be true after all — and we can learn them not only from our own dads, but from all the men who influence our outlook on the world.

This book contains some of those wise words passed down through generations of fathers to their children. They prove once again, as Dad might say, "You can learn a lot from those who have gone before you." And, you know... he'd be right!

"Don't count the days;
make the days count."

Always take time for...

Big smiles. Sunday mornings. Long walks.
Warm appreciation. Precious memories.
Things that bring a sense of joy to your heart.
Staying in touch... with the people who will
always mean so much.

Find a way to...

Be good to yourself (really good). Build the
bridges that will take you everywhere you've
ever wanted to go. Write out your own
definition of success, and then do your
absolute best to make that story come true.
Get closer and closer to the summit of every
mountain you've ever wanted to climb.
Make the most... of your moment...
of this moment in time.

Make plans to...

Slow down the days. Find your perfect
pace. Be strong enough. Be gentle enough.
Reap the sweet rewards that will come from
all the good things you do and all the great
things you give. Keep things in perspective.

Remember to...

Invest wisely in the best riches of all.
Share invaluable words over warm cups in
quiet places. Treasure time spent in heart-
to-heart conversations. Laugh a lot. Work
it all out. Move ahead of every worry.
Move beyond any sorrows. Have yourself
a wealth of beautiful tomorrows.

And (last, but not least)
never underestimate
the power of...

Friendship. Family. Chocolate.
And love.

———————————
Douglas Pagels

"Begin where you are...
but don't stay there."

Expect the best of yourself. Imagine that you have unlimited potential and that you can accomplish anything that you put your mind to. Imagine that your future is limited only by your own imagination and that whatever you have accomplished up to now is only a small part of what you are truly capable of achieving. Imagine that your greatest moments lie ahead and that everything that has happened to you up to now has merely been preparation for the great things that are yet to come.

Brian Tracy

Twenty years from now you will be more disappointed by the things you didn't do than by the ones you did do. So throw off the bowlines. Sail away from the safe harbor. Catch the trade winds in your sails. Explore. Dream. Discover.

Mark Twain

Go forward with large confidence and high expectation. Be alert to the fresh opportunities of this day and do everything possible to advance your highest and best interests. Stimulate your mind with clear, strong, uplifting ideas of what you wish to accomplish. Realize the immense powers and resources at your personal command. Make this day mark a distinct and important advance in your progress toward a great life ideal.

Grenville Kleiser

"When opportunity knocks...
answer right away."

The golden opportunity you are seeking is
in yourself. It is not in your environment;
it is not in luck or chance or the help of
others; it is in yourself alone.

Orison Swett Marden

Sing a new song; dance a new step; take a new path.
Think a new thought; accept a new responsibility;
memorize a new poem. Try a new recipe; plan a new
adventure; entertain a new idea. Learn a new language;
blaze a new trail; enjoy a new experience. Make a new
friend; read a new book; see a new movie. Climb a
new hill; scale a new mountain; launch a new career.
Find a new purpose; fill a new need; light a new lamp.
Exercise a new strength; grasp a new truth; practice a
new awareness. Add a new dimension; encourage a new
growth; affirm a new beginning. Discover a new answer;
envision a new image; conceive a new system. Dream a
new dream; chart a new course; build a new life. Open
a new door; explore a new possibility; capture a new
vision. Start a new chapter; seek a new challenge;
express a new confidence. Write a new plan; turn a
new page; follow a new direction. Watch a new
program; be a new person; radiate a new enthusiasm.

William Arthur Ward

"Don't put off until tomorrow
what you can do today."

Today is, for all that we know, the opportunity and occasion of our lives. On what we do or say today may depend the success and completeness of our entire life-struggle. It is for us, therefore, to use every moment of today as if our very eternity were dependent on its words and deeds.

Henry Clay Trumbull

Winners know that today is the day that counts. Today is the time to live with class, with confidence, with courage, and with character. Today is the day to achieve greatness, if only in small things. The real winners in life know that success is a skill, and they practice every day so that when the big challenges and extraordinary opportunities arrive, they are prepared.

Philip Humbert

We shall never have more time. We have, and have always had, all the time there is. No object is served in waiting until next week or even until tomorrow. Keep going day in and day out. Concentrate on something useful. Having decided to achieve a task, achieve it at all costs.

Arnold Bennett

"Actions speak louder than words."

❧

Hold yourself responsible for a higher standard than anybody else expects of you.

Henry Ward Beecher

Character is not something you were born with and can't change, like your fingerprint. In fact, because you weren't born with it, it is something that you must take responsibility for creating.... Character is built by how you respond to what happens in your life. Whether it's winning every game or losing every game. Getting rich or dealing with hard times. You build character out of certain qualities that you must create and diligently nurture within yourself. Just like you would plant and water a seed or gather wood and build a campfire. You've got to look for those things in your heart and in your gut. You've got to chisel away in order to find them. Just like chiseling away the rock in order to create the sculpture that has previously existed only in your imagination.

Jim Rohn

"Be the best of whatever you are."

Open the door to beautiful possibilities.
Close out the stress and the woes.
Be sure to invite the wonder in
    and let the worries go.

Think of each day as a treasured gift,
    and give that gift your best.
Accomplish those things
    that are in your power.
(Don't worry about the rest.)

Do a world of good in a world that
needs all the good it can get.
During the course of each day, come
    closer to goals, dreams,
        and challenges met.

Take or make the time to do what
you've always wanted to do. Choose
the paths that will make your heart glad.
Try to get to a place where you can live
the life you've always wanted to have.

Remember the saying, "It's nice
to be important, but it's more
important to be nice." Remember:
Every good choice has a reward.
Every bad choice has a price.

It's a difficult world we live in, but
don't let anything tarnish your star.
Wonderful things come to people
who... are as wonderful
as you are.

———————————

Douglas Pagels

"It's all up to you."

The best day of your life is the one on which you decide your life is your own. No apologies or excuses. No one to lean on, rely on, or blame. The gift is yours — it is an amazing journey — and you alone are responsible for the quality of it. This is the day your life really begins.

Bob Moawad

Always bear in mind that your own resolution to succeed is more important than any other one thing.

Abraham Lincoln

If you want to succeed in the world you must make your own opportunities as you go on. The man who waits for some seventh wave to toss him on dry land will find that the seventh wave is a long time a-coming. You can commit no greater folly than to sit by the road side until someone comes along and invites you to ride with him to wealth or influence.

John Bartholomew Gough

"Love is the key that unlocks every door."

There is nothing in this world more beautiful than love. It touches a heart and turns it into a temple. It lifts a soul toward heaven and makes each one of us better when we give ourselves to it.

Love fills the world with virtue, courage, sacrifice, thoughtfulness, and good works. Without these, the world would not be a suitable place for us to dwell in.

Love creates a more congenial and peaceful atmosphere that is most conducive to enjoying a fuller and more noble existence. To dedicate one's life to love is to live the best way for ourselves and others. There is no higher calling than to give love; there is no greater blessing than to receive it.

Daniel Haughian

"True love is worth waiting for."

———— ❧ ————

True love is being the best of friends — being able to say and share anything while still being sensitive to the other's feelings.

True love is built upon complete trust — complete by knowing that you can never be deceitful or misleading, because to do so would forever cloud the relationship with doubt.

True love is knowing that you'd rather be with this other person than with anyone else, and you feel a sense of emptiness when the two of you are apart.

It's when you always think of the future in terms of "we" instead of "me."

It is knowing that life will bring pain and sorrow, but together, you will support each other and overcome even the most difficult times.

True love is showing and saying "I love you" even when you both know — through a simple smile — that doing so isn't necessary.

True love is complete within itself, and it lasts into eternity.

Tim Tweedie

"Keep friends close to your heart."

Friends are together when they are separated, they are rich when they are poor, strong when they are weak, and — a thing even harder to explain — they live on after they have died, so great is the honor that follows them, so vivid the memory, so poignant the sorrow.

Cicero

There is nothing on this earth more to be prized than true friendship.

St. Thomas Aquinas

People who have warm friends are healthier and happier than those who have none. A single friend is a treasure worth more than gold or precious stones. Money can buy many things, good and evil. All the wealth of the world could not buy you a friend or pay you for the loss of one.

C. D. Prentice

If instead of a gem, or even a flower, we should cast the gift of a loving thought into the heart of a friend, that would be giving as the angels give.

George E. MacDonald

"No act of kindness, however small, is ever wasted."

It's what each of us sows, and how, that gives to us character and prestige. Seeds of kindness, goodwill, and human understanding, planted in fertile soil, spring up into deathless friendships, big deeds of worth, and a memory that will not soon fade.

George Matthew Adams

How far you go in life depends on you being tender with the young, compassionate with the aged, sympathetic with the striving, and tolerant of the weak and the strong. Because someday in life you will have been all of these.

George Washington Carver

Do all the good you can,
By all the means you can,
In all the places you can,
At all the times you can,
To all the people you can,
As long as you ever can.

John Wesley

The best portion of a good man's life is his little, nameless, unremembered acts of kindness and love.

William Wordsworth

"Be a strong link
in the chain..."

Spend every day preparing for the next.

As you reach forward with one hand, accept the advice of those who have gone before you, and in the same manner reach back with the other hand to those who follow you; for life is a fragile chain of experiences held together by love. Take pride in being a strong link in that chain. Discipline yourself, but do not be harsh. The pleasures of life are yours to be taken. Share them with others, but always remember that you, too, have earned the right to partake.

Know those who love you; love is the finest of all gifts and is received only to be given. Embrace those who truly love you; for they are few in a lifetime. Then return that love tenfold, radiating it from your heart to fill their lives as sunlight warms the darkest corners of the earth. Love is a journey, not a destination; travel its path daily. Do this and your troubles will be as fleeting as footprints in the sand. When loneliness is your companion and all about you seems to be gone, pause and listen, for the sound of loneliness is silence, and in silence we hear best. Listen well, and your moments of silence will always be broken by the gentle words of encouragement spoken by those who love you.

Tim Murtaugh

"When the going gets tough, the tough get going."

Mental toughness is the ability to be at your best at all times, regardless of the circumstances. It's easy to do well when there's no pressure or stress, but how many of us can be poised when the heat is on? Mental toughness is constancy of purpose; it is total focus and emotional control. Mental toughness is not rigidity in the face of adversity; it's stability and poise in the face of challenge. Mental toughness is seeking out the corporate pressure that can't be avoided anyway and being energized by it. It's not the ability to survive a mistake or failure; it's the ability to come back even stronger from failure.

Mental toughness is not inherent. It's not something that people are born with. Instead, it's learned. We start small, achieving a minor goal. Then we set our sights higher and succeed again. We may not succeed each time, but if we work patiently toward our larger goals, savoring victories and shrugging off small setbacks, we will prevail. And each time we raise the ante, we gain skills and confidence that make the next success more likely.... This particular cycle — hard work, success, more hard work, more success, with the occasional setback thrown in — is the crucible of character.

Vince Lombardi, Jr.

27

"You could be the one who changes the world."

You could be the one
who makes the save,
stops the madness,
restores the peace.

You could be the one
who takes the heat
and endures the cold
to get the hard job done.

You could be the one
who upholds justice
and does so with dignity
and honor and integrity.

You could be the one
who is in the right place
at the right time
to make a major difference.

You could be the one
who tells the truth
that changes the world
when everyone recognizes it.

You could be the one
who makes the great art
that promotes beauty and grace
and expands conscience
    and consciousness.

You could be the one
who demonstrates real love,
defines true friendship...
and who gets everything you deserve.

———————————

Paul Hodges

"One man with courage makes a majority."

———————— ❧ ————————

Whatever you do, you need courage. Whatever course you decide upon, there is always someone to tell you that you are wrong. There are always difficulties arising that tempt you to believe your critics are right. To map out a course of action and follow it to an end requires some of the same courage that a soldier needs. Peace has its victories, but it takes brave men and women to win them.

———————

Ralph Waldo Emerson

We should replace fear with courage, regression with progress, pride with humility, lethargy and inaction with ambition and activity. You need imagination, golden dreams, new horizons, unlimited panoramas, vision. May you never fail to thrill at the twinkling of a star, at the unfolding of the petals of a rose, at the sudden birth of a new idea. Fear not that your life shall come to an end, but rather that it shall never have a beginning.

———————

John Henry Newman

Be strong... the one thing that really matters is to be bigger than the things that can happen to you. Nothing that can happen to you is half so important as the way in which you meet it.

———————

Anonymous

31

"Challenge yourself. You may be surprised by what you can achieve."

In order to live a dream, you must first reach for it. You must go after dreams... with one hundred percent full commitment, heart, and soul. It takes courage to go after lofty aspirations, especially if they seem impossible at the time. If you desire to do or experience something new for the first time, let nothing impede your forward progress. To realize honorable, pure, and noble dreams, you first have to go for them.

Milton Willis and Michael Willis

It is not because things are difficult
that we do not dare. It is because we
do not dare that they are difficult.

Seneca

Whatever you can do or dream you can do, begin it.
Boldness has genius and magic and power in it.

Johann Wolfgang von Goethe

There is no planet, sun, or star that could
hold you if you but knew who you are.

Ralph Waldo Emerson

"Always go the extra mile."

When you do the common things in life in an uncommon way, you will command the attention of the world.

George Washington Carver

A man who does a little more work than he's asked to — who takes a little more care than he's expected to — who puts the small details on an equal footing with the more important ones — he's the one who is going to make a success of his job. Each little thing done better is the thin end of the wedge into something bigger.

Author Unknown

The heights by great men reached and kept were not attained by sudden flight, but they, while their companions slept, were toiling upward in the night.

Henry Wadsworth Longfellow

I would rather be ashes than dust! I would rather that my spark should burn out in a brilliant blaze than it should be stifled by dry rot. I would rather be a superb meteor, every atom of me in magnificent glow, than a sleepy and permanent planet. The proper function of man is to live, not to exist. I shall not waste my days in trying to prolong them. I shall use my time.

Jack London

"Choose a job you love, and you will never have to work a day in your life."

❧

Whatever you do, do it with all your might. Work at it, early and late, in season and out of season, not leaving a stone unturned, and never deferring for a single hour that which can be done just as well now.

P.T. Barnum

Every job is a self-portrait of the person who does it. Autograph your work with excellence.

Author Unknown

If you aim for a large, broad-gauged success, do not begin your business career, whether you sell your labor or are an independent producer, with the idea of getting from the world by hook or crook all you can. In the choice of your profession or business employment, let your first thought be: Where can I fit in so that I may be most effective in the work of the world? Where can I lend a hand in a way most effectively to advance the general interests? Enter life in such a spirit, choose your vocation in that way, and you have taken the first step on the highest road to a large success.

John D. Rockefeller

"Never get so busy making a living that you forget to make a life."

All our lives long, we hear the quiet advice, "Life is short. Make the most of it." And, deep in our hearts we know... that there really is a lot of wisdom behind those words.

But in the rush-a-day world we live in, where we get swamped by busy schedules and distracted by all the responsibilities placed upon us, it is so easy to forget the wisdom and the warmth of that advice.

We all have times when we need a reminder... a message to bring us back to the center; a maxim to help us bear in mind what's really important; a few encouraging words to nourish our souls and help us envision the big picture rather than simply focusing in on the minor details and major distractions.

Everyone has their ups and downs. And at times, the roller coaster ride we're on is a little scarier than we'd like it to be. But in the end, what's important is that we have a ticket to go on this journey. We are given the absolutely incredible gift of a new sunrise each and every morning. A new day! A new way of doing things. A chance to turn ordinary into extraordinary. An opportunity to get — even if it's only one little step — a little closer to our dreams, our hopes, our favorite people, and our most wonderful wishings.

And yes, maybe life is short. But when we slow down and take the time, we can't help but find... that it's very big on blessings.

Douglas Pagels

"What's the rush?"

❧

A sense of urgency is useful, valuable, to be desired, and encouraged. Yet there's a big difference between working with urgency and rushing through your work.

Yes, you want to get it done as quickly as possible. You also want to get it done right. Because getting it wrong and having to start over will cause an even bigger delay than taking the time to do it right.

Focus on what you're doing. Put the worries or excitement about what's coming next out of your mind. Give your full attention to the task at hand. Take the time to do it right, so you won't have to do it again.

If you've tried speeding up and it doesn't seem to get you anywhere, consider slowing down. Speed is not the only thing that matters. Quality matters. Effectiveness matters. Paying attention matters. If you were having surgery, would you want the surgeon to rush through the operation?

Respect what you're doing enough to give it the time and attention it deserves, and see how much more you can accomplish.

Ralph Marston

"Winning is about more than who comes in first."

❦

Throughout your life, you will face many challenges in your personal and public worlds; you will experience defeats as well as victories. How you handle those inevitable setbacks will probably play a more significant role in your destiny than your moments of success. In the end, your attitude is more important than whether you actually win or lose...

When you have a winning attitude, negativity cannot influence your outlook on the future. Even in the aftermath of setbacks and disappointment your confidence quickly regains its stride, because you're so determined to make progress every day. You're comfortable taking paths that may lead you away from the crowd, because you measure success by no one's standards but your own.

With a winning attitude, you realize that you're in control of your moods and emotions. You cannot choose what happens to you but you do decide how to respond — and with those choices, you build the integrity, balance, and judgment that shape your own soul as well as the world around you. When you know in your heart that winning is about more than just coming in first... you are ready for the kind of success achieved by only the very few.

Jon Peyton

"There's strength in numbers."

Ultimately, the greatest achievements in our lives come about as the result of teamwork. With the right group of people, there are no limits to what you can strive for; you can literally change the world in positive and profound ways.

Gary Morris

It is one of the beautiful compensations of this life that no one can sincerely try to help another without helping himself.

Charles Dudley Warner

Cooperation between members of a team — forged in the arena of competition found in every field of endeavor — supercharges the evolution of each individual's abilities. Cooperation enables them to transform themselves in ways that might otherwise be impossible.

Mitchell Lawes

Keep away from people who try to belittle your ambitions. Small people will always do that, but the really great make you feel that you, too, can become great.

Mark Twain

"One person can make a difference."

⚜

One person in the right can make all
the difference in a world gone wrong.

Milton Willis and Michael Willis

If you would find greater joy in life, attempt to
serve and please someone every day. The gift of
yourself to someone who needs you will, in return,
bring the gift of confidence and serenity to you.

John H. Crowe

I count that day as wisely spent in which I do some good
for someone who is far away... or shares my neighborhood.
A day devoted to the deed that lends a helping hand and
demonstrates a willingness to care and understand. I long to
be of usefulness in little ways and large, without a selfish
motive and without the slightest charge — because in my
philosophy there never is a doubt that all of us here on
earth must help each other out. I feel that day is fruitful,
and the time is worth the while, when I promote the
happiness of one enduring smile.

Author Unknown

"Look on the bright side."

Welcome every morning with a smile. Look on the new day as another special gift from your Creator, another golden opportunity to complete what you were unable to finish yesterday. Be a self-starter. Let your first hour set the theme of success and positive action that is certain to echo through your entire day. Today will never happen again. Don't waste it with a false start or no start at all. You were not born to fail.

Og Mandino

One thing is sure: You can't have darkness and light in the same place at the same time. The cure for a gloomy outlook is a lighted mind.

A. P. Gouthey

Be so strong that nothing can disturb your peace of mind. Talk health, happiness, and prosperity to every person you meet. Make all your friends feel there is something in them. Look at the sunny side of everything. Think only of the best, work only for the best, and expect only the best. Be as enthusiastic about the success of others as you are about your own. Forget the mistakes of the past and press on to the greater achievements of the future. Give everyone a smile. Spend so much time improving yourself that you have no time left to criticize others. Be too big for worry and too noble for anger.

Christian D. Larsen

"Always hope for the best."

—⚘—

As long as you have hope... you have direction,
the energy to move, and the map to move by.
You have a hundred alternatives, a thousand paths,
and an infinity of dreams. Hopeful, you are
halfway to where you want to go.

Anonymous

The men whom I have seen succeed best in life have always
been cheerful and hopeful men, who went about their
business with a smile on their faces, and took the changes
and chances of this mortal life like men, facing rough and
smooth alike as it came.

Charles Kingsley

Hope sees the invisible, feels the
intangible, and achieves the impossible.

Charles Caleb Colton

Always expect the best. Then, if you have to hurdle a few
tough problems, you will have generated the strength and
courage to do so.

George Matthew Adams

"Attitude is everything."

Positive thinkers get positive results because they appreciate the inestimable value of a day, this day, not the next day, but <u>this</u> day, and every day. Today offers at least sixteen waking hours that may be crammed full of opportunity, joy, excitement, achievement. The positive thinker knows that today was made for him and for everyone who will go for it positively. Today is his, so he makes it a marvelous creative experience. The positive thinker's optimistic attitude toward today and every succeeding day strongly tends to make every day a great day. It becomes what he visualizes it to be.

Norman Vincent Peale

We cannot choose how many years we will live, but we can choose how much life those years will have. We cannot control the beauty of our face, but we can control the expression on it. We cannot control life's difficult moments but we can choose to make life less difficult. We cannot control the negative atmosphere of the world, but we can control the atmosphere of our minds. Too often we try to choose and control things we cannot. Too seldom we choose to control what we can... our attitude.

Author Unknown

"Keep it simple."

❧

The trouble with so many of us is that we underestimate the power of simplicity. We have a tendency, it seems, to over-complicate our lives and forget what's important and what's not. We tend to mistake movement for achievement. We tend to focus on activities instead of results. And as the pace of life continues to race along in the outside world, we forget that we have the power to control our lives regardless of what's going on outside.

Robert Stuberg

If you want to be free, learn to
live simply. Use what you have
and be content where you are.

J. Heider

To find the universal elements enough; to find the air and the water exhilarating; to be refreshed by a morning walk or an evening saunter... to be thrilled by the stars at night; to be elated over a bird's nest or a wildflower in spring — these are some of the rewards of the simple life.

John Burroughs

"Money can't buy you happiness."

To be rich in admiration and free from envy; to rejoice greatly in the good of others; to love with such generosity of heart that your love is still a dear possession in absence. These are the gifts of fortune which money cannot buy, and without which money can buy nothing.

Robert Louis Stevenson

In the end it is not the one who keeps, but the one who gives away, who is rich; and it is giving away, not possession, which renders a man happy.

Clement of Alexandria

Time is infinitely more precious than money, and there is nothing common between them. You cannot accumulate time; you cannot borrow time; you can never tell how much time you have left in the Bank of Life. Time is life...

Israel Davidson

It is not how much we have, but how much we enjoy, that makes happiness.

Charles Haddon Spurgeon

"You <u>can</u> take it with you!"

---- ❧ ----

When you leave your home in the morning you take yourself with you. You take with you all that you have become, all that you are. If you want to find joy, love, peace, courage, faith, you must take them with you in your mind and heart.

When you step forth to meet your day there is more involved than your body. Your thoughts step forth, too. Your spirit also moves out into life. All that you have thought, and read, prayed for and meditated about, all the impressions that you have received are a part of the <u>you</u> that faces the world.

What you are flows from you to others. You project yourself. People tune in on the frequencies on which you vibrate. The qualities you project will determine the responses you receive. The outer world you experience will be determined by the inner world you take with you.

You can take it with you. There is no way in which you can avoid taking with you what you are.

Wilferd A. Peterson

"Be thankful for what you have."

Be thankful that you don't already have
everything you desire.
If you did, what would there be to look forward to?

Be thankful when you don't know something,
For it gives you the opportunity to learn.
Be thankful for the difficult times.
During those times you grow.

Be thankful for your limitations
Because they give you opportunities for improvement.
Be thankful for each new challenge
Because it will build your strength and character.

Be thankful for your mistakes;
They will teach you valuable lessons.
Be thankful when you're tired and weary
Because it means you've made a difference.

It is easy to be thankful for the good things.
A life of rich fulfillment comes to those who are
   also thankful for the setbacks.
Gratitude can turn a negative into a positive.
Find a way to be thankful for your troubles
and they can become your blessings.

Author Unknown

"Learn from your mistakes."

If I had a formula for bypassing trouble, I would not pass it around. Trouble creates a capacity to handle it. I don't embrace trouble; that's as bad as treating it as an enemy. But I do say: meet it as a friend, for you'll see a lot of it, and had better be on speaking terms with it.

Oliver Wendell Holmes

My great concern is not whether you have failed, but whether you are content with your failure.

Abraham Lincoln

It is a mistake to suppose that men succeed through success; they much oftener succeed through failures. Precept, study, advice, and example could never have taught them so well as failure has done.

Samuel Smiles

"Everything in life is a teacher."

Before this day ends, I guarantee life will give you the opportunity to learn something about yourself. Life is an interesting and fascinating series of events, processes, and growth opportunities. It is what happens to us as we plan the outcomes of our life existence. Life is truly a classroom. In a sense, class begins the day we are born, and ends the day we pass from this world to the next. There are no vacations, recesses, and you never graduate.

There is no final exam and there is no pass or fail. You can, however, repeat a grade again and again, until you learn the necessary skills or attitudes that the teachers in this class are trying to help you learn. Each of us is traveling through our very unique lives toward a variety of circumstances, events, people, and outcomes. We are bringing these outcomes and people into our lives both unconsciously and consciously.

Some people are good students, and learn the necessary lessons the first time they appear, while others are stuck in the same old patterns, life dramas, and situations, because they fail to bring the learning back to themselves. You can't quit school, and you must complete each assignment before you get to move on to the next one. Some people refuse to see the learning as theirs.

The opportunity for learning can be found from each of life's experiences or teachers. The key to happiness is to learn to bring all of the learning back to yourself, and not to point your finger at others. We don't get to choose the curriculum in our lives, or the lives of others.

Tim Connor

"The road to success is always under construction."

❧

The most successful men in the end are those whose success is the result of steady accretion.... It is the man who carefully advances step by step, with his mind becoming wider and wider — and progressively better able to grasp any theme or situation — persevering in what he knows to be practical, and concentrating his thought upon it, who is bound to succeed in the greatest degree.

Alexander Graham Bell

Luck is always waiting for something to turn up. Labor, with keen eyes and strong will, always turns up something. Luck lies in bed and wishes the postman will bring news of a legacy. Labor turns out at six o'clock and with busy pen or ringing hammer, lays the foundation of a competence. Luck whines. Labor whistles. Luck relies on chance, labor on character.

Richard Cobden

There are two kinds of success. One is the very rare kind that comes to the man who has the power to do what no one else has the power to do. That is genius. But the average man who wins what we call success is not a genius. He is a man who has merely the ordinary qualities that he shares with his fellows, but who has developed those ordinary qualities to a more than ordinary degree.

Theodore Roosevelt

"Keep everything in perspective."

We're here for a moment in time — and then we're gone. Why waste one second on self-pity, frustration, irritation, and all the rest? Our lives are so much more important than that.

It's shocking what happens to the quality of your life when you put it into this perspective. All of a sudden, the things that seemed so big seem small. And the things that seemed so small — and the things we postpone and take for granted — seem so big! We see that, for the most part, we usually prioritize in reverse order. But we can change all that in a moment. We can make a shift right now.

The things that we so often attach importance to are important, but it's a question of degree. Success, perfection, achievement, money, recognition — you can have them all, but they're not everything. In fact, without a passion and appreciation for life, they don't amount to much.

Richard Carlson

Take life too seriously, and what is it worth? If the morning wakes us to no new joys, if the evening brings us not the hopes of new pleasures, is it worth while to dress and undress? Does the sun shine on me today that I may reflect on yesterday? That I may endeavor to foresee and control what can neither be foreseen nor controlled — the destiny of tomorrow?

Johann Wolfgang von Goethe

"Life is 10 percent what you make it and 90 percent how you take it."

---- 🌿 ----

It isn't what you have or who you are or where you are
or what you are doing that makes you happy or unhappy.
It is what you think about it. For example, two people
may be in the same place, doing the same thing; both may
have about an equal amount of money and prestige —
and yet one may be miserable and the other happy.
Why? Because of a different mental attitude.

Dale Carnegie

One of the valid ways to test your attitude is to answer this
question: "Do you feel your world is treating you well?" If your
attitude toward the world is excellent, you will receive excellent
results. If you feel so-so about the world, your response from
the world will be average. Feel badly about your world, and
you will seem to have only negative feedback from life. Look
around you. Analyze the conversations of people who lead
unhappy, unfulfilled lives. You will find they are crying against a
society which they feel is out to get them and to give them a
lifetime of trouble, misery, and bad luck. Sometimes the prison
of discontent has been built by their own hands.

The world doesn't care whether we free ourselves from this
prison or not. It marches on. Adopting a good, healthy attitude
toward life does not affect society nearly so much as it affects
us. The change cannot come from others. It must come from us.

John C. Maxwell

"You can go as far as your dreams will take you."

You have the ability to attain
whatever you seek; within you
is every potential you can imagine.
Always aim higher than
you believe you can reach.
So often, you'll discover
you can achieve any goal.
If people offer you their help or wisdom
as you go through life,
accept it gratefully.
You can learn much from those
who have gone before you.
But never be afraid or hesitant
to step off the accepted path
and strike off on your own,
if your heart tells you it's right.
Regard failure as a perfect opportunity
to show yourself how strong you truly are.
Believe in persistence, discipline,
   and always believe in yourself.
You are meant to be
      whatever you dream of becoming.

Edmund O'Neill

"Let your heart be your compass."

Life is a journey with many paths
   to choose from —
but the one path that leads to life
   and true fulfillment
is one that only the heart can know.
Let your heart be your compass;
   it knows the right road for you.
The mind can be filled with many voices
   that beckon you to follow the world.
These may seem logical, but it is
   <u>not</u> the road of your calling.
You are born for a purpose —
   a plan only you can fulfill —
and this plan has its own special path
if it is ever to be walked on and lived.

Life has many pitfalls and can be filled
    with tragedies,
so take the time to look within
    and follow your heart —
no matter what the cost.
It is your road of life.
The heart is the divine connection
that can see the dangers ahead
    and keep you on the straight highway
        made just for you.
You will know it is from the heart
    if you have inner peace.
So look to your heart every day,
    in every way and decision.
Life is a choice that leads
    into eternity,
so choose carefully...
    and follow your heart.

———————

Dan Lynch

"Life is an adventure... make the most of it!"

❧

Nobody ever said that it would be easy, or that the skies would always be sunny. When gray days and worrisome times come along, you need to stay strong. Know that everything will be okay...

Leave behind the little worries. Tomorrow they won't matter, and next month you may not even remember what they were. Take the others <u>one at a time</u>, and you'll be amazed at how your difficulties manage to become easier.

Find your smile. Warm yourself with your quiet determination and your knowledge of brighter days ahead. Do the things that need to be done. Say the words that need to be said.

Happiness is waiting for you. Believe in your ability. Cross your bridges. Listen to your heart. Your faith in tomorrow will <u>always</u> help you do what is right, and it will help you be strong along the path of life.

———

Collin McCarty

ACKNOWLEDGMENTS

We gratefully acknowledge the permission granted by the following authors, publishers, and authors' representatives to reprint poems or excerpts from their publications.

Berrett-Koehler Publishers, San Francisco, CA, www.bkconnection.com, for "Expect the best of yourself..." from THE 100 ABSOLUTELY UNBREAKABLE LAWS OF BUSINESS SUCCESS by Brian Tracy. Copyright © 2000 by Brian Tracy. Reprinted by permission of the publisher. All rights reserved.

Dr. Philip E. Humbert for "Winners know that today...." Copyright © 2005 by Philip Humbert. All rights reserved.

Jim Rohn for "Character is not something..." from *Jim Rohn Weekly E-zine*, www.jimrohn.com (Issue 97, August 21, 2001). Copyright © 2001 by Jim Rohn. All rights reserved.

Bob Moawad for "The best day of your life...." Copyright © 2003 by Bob Moawad. All rights reserved.

Daniel Haughian for "There is nothing in this world...." Copyright © 2005 by Daniel Haughian. All rights reserved.

The McGraw-Hill Companies for "Mental toughness is..." from WHAT IT TAKES TO BE #1 by Vince Lombardi, Jr. Copyright © 2001 by Vince Lombardi, Jr. All rights reserved.

Paul Hodges for "You could be the one...." Copyright © 2005 by Paul Hodges. All rights reserved.

Milton Willis and Michael Willis for "In order to live a dream..." and "One person in the right...." Copyright © 2005 by Milton Willis and Michael Willis. All rights reserved.

The Daily Motivator for "What's the rush?" by Ralph S. Marston, Jr. Copyright © 2001 by Ralph S. Marston, Jr. Used by permission. Originally published in *The Daily Motivator* at www.dailymotivator.com (March 30, 2001). All rights reserved.

Bantam Books, a division of Random House, Inc., for "Welcome every morning..." from A BETTER WAY TO LIVE by Og Mandino. Copyright © 1990 by Og Mandino. All rights reserved.

Thomas Nelson Publishers, Inc., Nashville, TN., for "Positive thinkers get..." from WHY SOME POSITIVE THINKERS GET POWERFUL RESULTS by Norman Vincent Peale. Copyright © 1986 by Norman Vincent Peale. All rights reserved. And for "One of the valid ways..." from THE WINNING ATTITUDE by John C. Maxwell. Copyright © 1993 by John C. Maxwell. All rights reserved.

Robert Stuberg for "The trouble with so many...." Copyright © 1997 by Robert Stuberg. All rights reserved.

Heacock Literary Agency for "You can take it with you!" from THE ART OF LIVING, DAY BY DAY by Wilferd A. Peterson, published by Simon & Schuster. Copyright © 1972 by Wilferd A. Peterson. All rights reserved.

Tim Connor for "Everything in life is a teacher" from THE ROAD TO HAPPINESS IS FULL OF POTHOLES. Copyright © 1997 by Tim Connor. All rights reserved.

Theodore Roosevelt Association for "There are two kinds of success..." by Theodore Roosevelt. Copyright © 1913 by Theodore Roosevelt. All rights reserved.

Hyperion for "We're here for a moment in time..." from DON'T SWEAT THE SMALL STUFF FOR MEN by Richard Carlson, Ph.D. Copyright © 2001 by Richard Carlson, Ph.D. Reprinted by permission. All rights reserved.

Simon & Schuster for "It isn't what you have..." from HOW TO WIN FRIENDS AND INFLUENCE PEOPLE by Dale Carnegie. Copyright © 1936 by Dale Carnegie, copyright renewed © 1964 by Donna Dale Carnegie and Dorothy Carnegie. Revised Edition copyright © 1981 by Donna Dale Carnegie and Dorothy Carnegie. All rights reserved.

Dan Lynch for "Life is a journey...." Copyright © 2005 by Dan Lynch. All rights reserved.

A careful effort has been made to trace the ownership of selections used in this anthology in order to obtain permission to reprint copyrighted material and give proper credit to the copyright owners. If any error or omission has occurred, it is completely inadvertent, and we would like to make corrections in future editions provided that written notification is made to the publisher:

BLUE MOUNTAIN ARTS, INC., P.O. Box 4549, Boulder, Colorado 80306.